Action for the Environment

Energy Supplies

Chris Oxlade

W
FRANKLIN WATTS
LONDON • SYDNEY

© 2004 Franklin Watts

Franklin Watts
96 Leonard Street
London EC2A 4XD

Franklin Watts Australia
45–51 Huntley Street
Alexandria
NSW 2015

ISBN: 0 7496 5537 2

A CIP catalogue record for this book is
available from the British Library

Printed in Malaysia

Editor: Adrian Cole
Design: Proof Books
Art Director: Jonathan Hair
Picture Research: Kathy Lockley

Acknowledgements
The publishers would like to thank the
following for permission to reproduce
photographs in this book:

AA World Travel Library 19 t. Argus/Still Pictures 4. Blue
Energy Canada, www.bluenergy.com 19 b. William
Campbell/Still Pictures Cover tl. Vicki Coombs/Ecoscene
10. Anthony Cooper/Ecoscene 20. © Digital Vision Ltd. All
rights reserved 8. Mark Edwards/Still Pictures 17 b. Courtesy
Energy Efficiency 25 b. © Copyright European Commission
27 bc. Geo-Heat Center, Photo by John Lund 22.
Greenpeace UK 7 b. Chinch Gryniewicz /Ecoscene Cover b,
16, 24. Angela Hampton/Ecoscene Cover tr. Robert Harding
Picture Library 28. ITDG/ZUL 21 t, /Marie Jose-Perez 18.
Japan Information & Cultural Centre 23 b. David Hay
Jones/Science Photo Library 7 t. Kevin King/Ecoscene 23 t.
NQEA Australia Engineers and Shipbuilders 11. PA Photos
9. Ray Pfortner/Still Pictures 1, 6. © Copyright 1996
PhotoDisc, Inc. All rights reserved 12. Rex Features 29 t.
Kevin Schafer/Still Pictures 2, 15. Toyota GB 26. U.S. DOE
Photo 5, 13, 17 t, 21 b, 25 t, 27 bl. Jim Winkley/Ecoscene 14
b, 31. David Wootton/Ecoscene 14 t

Contents

Energy and our environment   4

What are energy supplies?   6

Stop the global disaster   8

Reducing pollution   10

Renewable energy supplies   12

Energy from the wind   14

Harnessing solar energy   16

Water energy   18

Organic energy   20

Energy from the ground   22

Keeping energy in   24

Energy-efficient machines   26

Stop throwing energy away   28

Glossary   30

Find out more   31

Index   32

Energy and our environment

By using fossil fuels, such as coal and gas, we have been harming our environment for more than 100 years. But other, more environmentally-friendly energy supplies are becoming available.

WE NEED ENERGY

Modern life involves using a lot of energy, and every year energy use increases. We use energy at home when we turn on a light. The machines we use, such as computers and televisions, need energy to work. Cars, buses and trains use energy to transport us from one place to another.

People in cities, like this one, use and waste lots of energy lighting and heating homes and offices.

DAMAGING THE ENVIRONMENT

Some ways of generating energy damage the environment more than others. The most harmful is the burning of fossil fuels, which produces pollution (see page 6). There are different forms of action being taken that will help to prevent bigger environmental problems in the future.

Action stations

One simple way we can help the environment is to use less energy. Remember to switch off electrical appliances fully. Some radios and televisions go on to 'stand-by' and keep using electricity even when they seem to be switched off! Ask your parents to fit energy-efficient light bulbs. Also, if your parents drive you to school in a car, ask them if you can ride with a friend or walk instead.

As well as changing our habits, we can also change the products we use. Using energy-efficient light bulbs, like these, means we use less energy.

TAKING ACTION

We can help the environment by changing the ways we generate and use energy, for example by using renewable energy supplies (see pages 12–13) and by not wasting energy. Scientists are also developing new energy supplies, such as 'cleaner' fuels for cars, which cause less damage to the environment.

What are energy supplies?

Fossil fuels are the main energy supply. They are used, for example, to power vehicles, cookers and heaters. Burning fossil fuels also generates most electricity, which is another energy supply. It is used to power electrical appliances.

BURNING FOSSIL FUELS

Fossil fuels are full of stored energy. To convert the energy they must be burned. Fossil fuels are called non-renewable energy supplies because once they have been completely burnt they cannot be used again. Burning fossil fuels also causes environmental pollution.

Burning fossil fuels at a power station, like this one, generates electricity. But fossil fuels are a non-renewable energy supply and eventually they will run out.

GENERATING ELECTRICITY

Electricity is generated at power stations, which need supplies of energy to convert into electricity. Most power stations around the world generate electricity by burning fossil fuels. However, in many countries, such as Sweden, electricity is also generated by using renewable energy supplies, which include flowing water (see pages 12–13). Unlike fossil fuels, renewable energy supplies will not run out.

This hydroelectric power station in Sweden generates electricity from flowing water energy.

Action stations

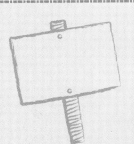

Greenpeace is an organisation that campaigns for governments around the world to make laws that protect the environment. One such campaign is Clean Energy Now! It calls for electricity supply companies to produce their electricity using fewer fossil fuels. It also asks local authorities to buy electricity produced using renewable supplies. Greenpeace has helped to persuade many city authorities to use more renewable energy supplies in the future.

Clean Energy Now! is one of many campaigns that Greenpeace runs to help protect the environment.

Stop the global disaster

When fossil fuels are burned, a gas called carbon dioxide is released into the air. Many governments are trying to reduce the level of carbon dioxide produced by the industries in their countries.

Global warming threatens to turn more areas of the world into desert.

GLOBAL WARMING

Over the last 100 years more people have used more fossil fuels to supply the energy they need. This has increased levels of carbon dioxide – a 'greenhouse gas' – in the Earth's atmosphere, which is trapping more of the Sun's heat and raising global temperatures. This is called global warming and it is the biggest environmental threat faced by the Earth.

GLOBAL EFFECTS

Most scientists think that global warming is already affecting the environment. Rising sea and air temperatures are slowly melting the ice in the Arctic and Antarctic. In the future, climate changes will probably cause more storms and droughts in different areas of the world.

More storms and hurricanes will occur as a result of climate changes.

TOUGH GLOBAL ACTION

Campaign groups, such as Friends of the Earth International (FoEI), are demanding tougher action to stop the Earth being damaged by global warming. FoEI are taking legal action to stop energy companies polluting the environment. They want to see companies developing and using renewable energy supplies that do not cause global warming (see page 12).

Action stations

In the 1990s, countries around the world began to take global warming seriously. In 1997, politicians from many countries met in Kyoto, Japan. They agreed to reduce greenhouse gas emissions by 2012. This is called the Kyoto Agreement. However, the USA, which produces one quarter of the world's greenhouse gas emissions, later rejected the agreement. Instead, it encourages companies to reduce emissions, but does not force them to do so.

This environmental protest was held during the 1997 meeting in Kyoto. All countries will have to reduce the amount of fossil fuels they burn in order to reverse global warming.

Reducing pollution

When fossil fuels are burned they produce other gas emissions. These pollute the atmosphere and cause breathing problems for many people. However, efforts are being made to reduce the levels of these emissions.

GAS EMISSIONS

Gas emissions often contain tiny drops of liquid and pieces of solid. These make the air look smoky. Some emissions, including nitrogen oxides, are poisonous. High levels of these in the air can make it difficult for some people to breathe.

IMPROVING TECHNOLOGY

The use of fossil fuels cannot suddenly stop, because at the moment renewable sources of energy are not used everywhere. However, new technology is helping to reduce the emissions of some fossil fuels. It is also reducing the amount of fossil fuel needed. Refineries can now remove most of the harmful sulphur from diesel fuel, while car engines are becoming more efficient so they burn less fuel.

Ultra Low Sulphur
Diesel BSEN 590

Low sulphur diesel and unleaded petrol are now widely available.

Action stations

Manufacturing industries create high levels of pollution and also use large amounts of electricity to make their products. In Australia, 375,000 businesses have signed up to the government's Environment Industry Action Agenda, which hopes to reduce energy use and cut pollution levels by encouraging companies to become more energy efficient.

Manufacturing industries in Australia are encouraged to reduce energy use and cut pollution levels.

Renewable energy supplies

Some energy comes from supplies that will never run out. These are called renewable energy supplies. Most of them do no damage at all to the environment. They are often called 'clean' or 'green' energy supplies.

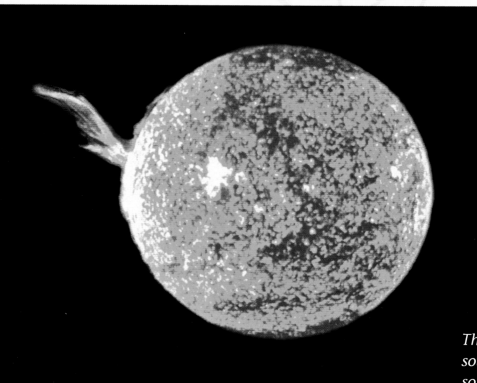

NATURAL ENERGY
The main renewable energy supplies are wind energy, solar energy, energy from flowing water (hydroelectricity), bioenergy and geothermal energy. All these supplies are natural, although to generate energy they have to be harnessed. For example, solar cells convert solar energy into electricity.

The Sun is the biggest source of renewable energy – solar power. If we harnessed just 1% of the Sun's energy that hits the Earth, all our energy needs would be met.

REDUCING POLLUTION
Using energy from a renewable supply is good for the environment. Energy supplied from a renewable source means that less energy is converted from fossil fuels, which means that less pollution goes into the atmosphere.

USING MORE RENEWABLE SOURCES

Since the beginning of the 1990s, more and more sources of renewable energy have been harnessed. This is because people have found better ways to generate renewable energy and it has become cheaper for people to use. For example, in 2003 people around the world used ten times as much wind energy as they did in 1992.

Action stations

Some electricity companies buy their supplies from renewable sources and belong to 'green power' schemes. People who buy electricity from them know they are using energy that has not been generated by burning fossil fuels. Ask your parents to find out if there is a green electricity scheme where you live.

Our electricity is supplied along cables. It is impossible to tell how the electricity has been generated unless we know more about the electricity supply company that uses the cables.

Energy from the wind

Wind energy is renewable because the wind will never stop blowing. Wind is the fastest-growing source of renewable energy. Experts think wind could produce 12% of the world's electricity by 2040.

WIND TURBINES

Machines called wind turbines harness wind energy. Most wind turbines have a rotor at the top of a mast, which can be up to 50 metres tall. The wind makes the rotor spin round slowly. The rotor turns a generator that converts the wind energy into electricity. A single wind turbine generates enough electricity for several hundred homes.

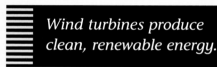

Wind turbines produce clean, renewable energy.

WIND FARMS

A collection of wind turbines is called a wind farm. Wind farms are only useful in places where it is windy all year round, such as Canada, Japan, the UK and the USA. A few hundred turbines produce as much electricity as a power station that burns fossil fuels.

A coastal wind farm in Copenhagen harbour, Denmark. Wind is the fastest-growing source of renewable energy.

Action stations

Denmark, in northern Europe, is a world leader in wind energy. About 7% of its electricity comes from wind turbines. By 2030 it plans to generate half of its electricity from wind energy. As well as large wind farms that make electricity for town and cities, there are individual turbines for farms and villages. Denmark also builds wind turbines for use in many other countries.

Wind farms, with hundreds of wind turbines, may eventually replace old-fashioned power stations that burn fossil fuels.

Harnessing solar energy

Energy comes from the Sun as heat and light. This is called solar energy. The use of solar energy is growing fast because it is clean, cheap and can be supplied to remote towns and villages.

SOLAR PANELS

A solar panel catches the Sun's heat and uses it to heat water for washing and bathing. Solar panels are a popular way of heating water in hot, sunny countries. They are simple and cheap to build.

SOLAR CELLS

A solar cell converts light into electricity. You may have a watch or calculator powered by electricity from a solar cell. One cell only generates a tiny amount of electricity. A solar array contains hundreds or thousands of cells. During the day it can generate enough electricity to meet the needs of a whole household.

This solar array converts light energy into electricity, which is used to power the lighthouse.

NEW CELL TECHNOLOGY

Older solar cells only convert about 15% of light energy into electricity, and they are also quite expensive. But new solar cells are more efficient and cheaper. Scientists have built cheap cells that convert 30% of light into electricity, which will make solar cells more popular.

SOLAR POWER STATIONS

At a solar power station, light and heat from the Sun are converted into electricity that is supplied to towns and cities. Japan and Germany are the largest producers of solar energy in the world.

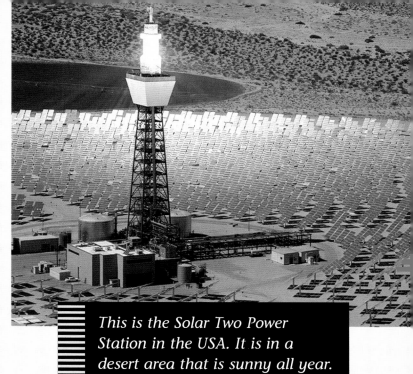

This is the Solar Two Power Station in the USA. It is in a desert area that is sunny all year.

Action stations

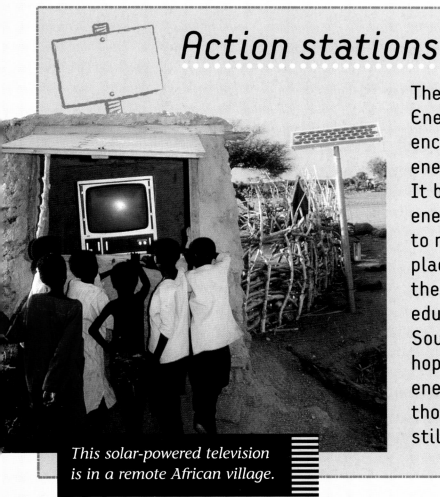

This solar-powered television is in a remote African village.

The International Solar Energy Society (ISES) encourages the use of solar energy around the world. It believes that renewable energy supplies will help to reduce poverty levels in places like Africa. Recently, the ISES has worked on educational programmes in South Africa and Kenya. It hopes to introduce solar energy to some of the thousands of homes there that still do not have electricity.

Water energy

People have been using flowing river water as a source of energy for thousands of years. Today, clean electricity is already generated by rivers. But scientists are finding ways to use energy from the oceans, too.

HYDROELECTRICITY

Hydroelectric power stations convert flowing water energy into electricity. River water flows through a dam into a turbine, making it spin. This turns a generator and produces electricity. Canada generates over 60% of its electricity in this way.

SMALL POWER STATIONS

Although big dams generate large amounts of electricity, they stop the natural flow of the river and create large lakes. This can harm water habitats and force people to move from the land that is flooded. Smaller 'micro-hydroelectric' power stations are being built instead. These still provide enough electricity for the needs of a village, factory or farm.

Micro-hydroelectric projects, like this one in Kenya, are becoming increasingly popular because they do very little damage to the surrounding environment.

ENERGY FROM THE SEA

Tides contain lots of energy. A dam called a tidal barrage harnesses tidal energy. It traps water at high tide and as the tide goes out, turbines in the barrage convert the flowing water energy into electricity.

This tidal barrage is on the River Rance in France.

Action stations

The Philippines is made up of many small islands. Strong currents flow through channels between the islands as the tide rises and falls. There are plans to build an underwater wall, called a tidal fence, between several islands in the San Bernardino passage in the Philippines. The fence will contain hundreds of turbines that will generate as much electricity as an enormous hydroelectric dam.

This is just one design idea for a tidal fence. The illustration shows the paddles that lie underwater and spin the turbines.

Organic energy

Bioenergy is an energy supply generated by some crops and biodegradable waste materials. It is renewable because new plants can be grown to replace the ones that are used. Bioenergy is a success story – millions of cars around the world are already powered by it.

BIOENERGY SUPPLIES

The materials that are used to generate bioenergy are called bioenergy feedstocks. Some crops are specially grown for bioenergy, while other biodegradable materials, such as old cardboard boxes, wood chippings and farm waste, are also used as bioenergy feedstocks.

This willow crop in Somerset, UK, is a bioenergy feedstock. It is being harvested so it can be burned to generate electricity.

GENERATING BIOENERGY

Some bioenergy feedstocks are burned in electricity generating stations, which reduces the use of fossil fuels. Some vegetables and plants are reduced to a liquid and converted into fuels, called biofuels. They are used instead of fossil fuels.

This small-scale biofuel plant is in Sri Lanka. Biofuel can be used to power machinery and cars.

CARBON DIOXIDE BALANCE

Unfortunately, burning biofuels releases carbon dioxide into the atmosphere. But plants use up carbon dioxide as they grow. So, new bioenergy crops that are planted balance the carbon dioxide levels in the atmosphere.

Action stations

Ethanol is the most widely used biofuel. It is made by reducing crops, such as sugar cane, potatoes and wheat, to a liquid, and only produces a tiny amount of pollution compared to petrol. Ethanol can be mixed with petrol and burned in a normal car engine. In Brazil, ethanol makes up 25% of all the car fuel used. Some Brazilian cars run on pure ethanol. In the USA, ethanol makes up 12% of car fuel.

An ethanol production plant in Illinois, USA. Pure ethanol is seen as the fuel of the future.

Energy from the ground

Beneath the Earth's surface lies hot, molten rock. The energy it contains is called geothermal energy. There is so much heat inside the Earth that it could be used for millions of years without running out. About 60 million people already use hot water or electricity supplied by geothermal energy.

GEOTHERMAL AREAS

In some countries, such as Iceland, New Zealand and Japan, there is a lot of molten rock near the Earth's surface. These are places where volcanoes and hot springs are common. Here it is quite easy to harness geothermal energy by pumping cold water down into the ground. The water is heated up quickly by the rock and comes back to the surface boiling hot.

The pools at this prawn farm in New Zealand are heated using hot water from the nearby geothermal plant.

USING GEOTHERMAL ENERGY

The hot water is piped from underground directly into houses to heat them up. For example, in Iceland every house is heated by hot water from geothermal supplies. The steam from the hot water is also used to drive generators that convert geothermal energy into electricity.

Laying hot water heating pipes under roads in Iceland helps to keep them ice-free.

Action stations

Japan has many volcanoes and hot springs and has been using geothermal energy since 1966, when the Matsukawa Geothermal Power Station opened. Japan now has 16 large geothermal power plants that generate electricity. Hot spring water is also used to warm homes, greenhouses, fish farms and swimming pools, and to stop roads getting icy in winter.

In Japan, geothermal power stations like this one provide thousands of homes and businesses with a renewable source of clean energy.

23

Keeping energy in

Every time we use energy supplies we do a small amount of damage to the environment. We cannot stop using energy, but we can stop wasting it by improving energy efficiency.

ESCAPING ENERGY

People who live in countries with a cold climate use a large amount of energy to heat their homes. Many of them stay warm by using electric heaters and burning fossil fuels. In old houses some of this precious energy escapes by accident and is wasted, but there are ways to stop this happening.

HEAT INSULATION

Modern houses have a layer of insulation in the walls and roof. The insulation stops warm air indoors touching the outside walls and roof, which would cool down the air indoors. Double-glazed windows help to stop heat escaping through the glass. Many countries have passed laws so that all new houses must have at least a minimum level of insulation.

Recycled paper pulp is sprayed into a wall cavity. This form of heat insulation will reduce energy wastage.

ENERGY-EFFICIENT BUILDINGS

Lots of energy is used to heat buildings in the winter and to air-condition them in the summer. Some modern buildings are cleverly designed to use less energy. Special glass can be fitted in windows to trap heat from the Sun on cold days and keep heat out on hot days.

This home has been designed to be as energy efficient as possible. Many people can get a grant to improve the energy efficiency of their own home.

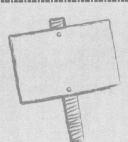

Action stations

Many governments run 'save energy' campaigns that encourage people to use energy sensibly and efficiently. They give people information about how to insulate their homes and how to buy appliances, such as washing machines, that do not waste energy. Some governments also help people on low incomes to pay to insulate their homes by providing grants.

ENERGY EFFICIENCY™

RECOMMENDED

Badges like this one help people to choose appliances that are energy efficient.

Energy-efficient machines

Many modern machines, from cars to kettles, are much more energy efficient than older machines. Buying an energy-efficient machine means that less energy is wasted.

The Toyota Prius is the most energy-efficient car ever mass-produced.

IMPROVED EFFICIENCY

New cars are becoming more energy efficient, and also cleaner. One of the most efficient and clean is the Toyota Prius. This car has a battery-powered electric motor and a petrol engine. At low speeds, the electric motor moves the car. At higher speeds, the petrol engine takes over and the battery recharges.

Action stations

Kitchen appliances made or sold in the European Union must by law display an energy label. The EU energy label rates the appliance from 'A' to 'G'. 'A' is the highest rating and means the appliance meets the highest energy-efficiency standards.

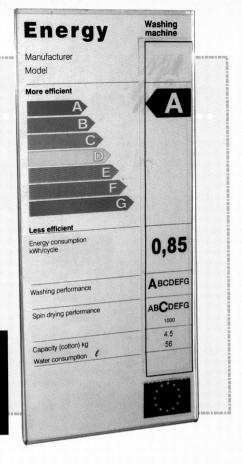

Energy		Washing machine
Manufacturer		
Model		

This label belongs to an 'A'-rated appliance. To attract more customers, manufacturers are always improving the energy efficiency of their machines.

EFFICIENT APPLIANCES

Domestic appliances, such as fridges, washing machines and televisions, use lots of electricity. Energy-efficient appliances are designed to waste as little energy as possible. For example, an energy-efficient fridge has excellent insulation so that no energy is wasted keeping it cool.

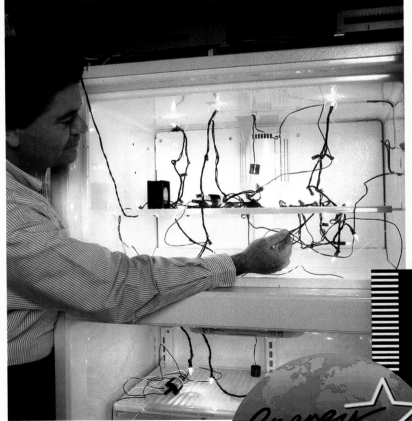

This scientist has adjusted this fridge so that it uses 50% less energy! Look out for energy-efficient appliances carrying the Energy Star logo.

Stop throwing energy away

Everything we use in our lives has been made somewhere. This manufacturing process uses vast amounts of energy and, if we throw things away after we have used them, the energy is wasted. We can save energy by re-using and recycling things.

THE DEMANDS OF INDUSTRY

We often forget about all the energy used by industries, such as electronics manufacturers and car assembly plants. They use enormous amounts of energy to make materials, such as metals and plastics, and even more energy is needed to power machines that turn these materials into objects.

The robots in this car plant may save time in the manufacturing process, but they use and waste a lot of energy.

RE-USING AND RECYCLING MATERIALS

Re-using and recycling materials saves manufacturing energy: making recycled paper uses 64% less energy than making new paper. Millions of people are already re-using and recycling, but more needs to be done. Some governments are now forcing people to recycle materials, such as glass and paper, by threatening to issue fines if they do not use their recycling collection bins. This will help save valuable energy supplies.

Action stations

Recycling is one of the simplest ways to save precious energy supplies and help the environment.
And it only takes a little bit of your own energy to do it! Make sure your household recycling collection box is used, or if you do not have one, make regular trips to your local recycling centre.

Recycling bins make it easier to sort out different materials, such as glass.

Glossary

Atmosphere The layer of air that surrounds the Earth.

Biodegradable When a material can be broken down naturally.

Bioenergy feedstocks Crops and materials used to generate bioenergy.

Biofuels Liquid fuels, including ethanol, converted from organic materials.

Campaign Action taken by a person or a group of people to try to persuade other people to change what they do.

Carbon dioxide The major greenhouse gas. Carbon dioxide is produced when fossil fuels are burned.

Efficiency A measure of how much energy a machine wastes as it does its job. An efficient machine uses less energy compared to an inefficient machine.

Emissions Waste gases, such as carbon dioxide, and tiny particles of solids that are discharged by vehicle engines and power stations where fuels are burned.

Environmental laws Laws that help to protect the environment.

Fossil fuels Fuels such as oil, natural gas and coal that are formed over millions of years from the remains of animals and plants.

Generator A device that produces electricity when its central section is turned at high speed.

Global warming The very gradual increase in the temperature of the Earth's atmosphere.

Grant Money given by a government, for example, to help people pay for something they cannot afford.

Greenhouse gases Gases, such as carbon dioxide, which are produced by burning fossil fuels.

Nitrogen oxides Nitrogen oxides come from burning fossil fuels in vehicles and power stations. They can seriously damage the environment.

Non-renewable energy supplies Energy supplies, such as oil and coal, that are gone forever when we use them.

Pollute To release harmful substances into the environment.

Recycling Using the material in an object to make a new object. For example, we can recycle glass in bottles to make new bottles.

Refinery A chemical plant where crude oil is split up into the different chemicals it contains, such as petrol and diesel oil.

Renewable energy supplies Energy supplies, such as wind energy and solar energy, that will never be used up. They cause little or no environmental damage.

Re-using Using something again rather than throwing it away after its first use. For example, we can re-use plastic bags until they wear out.

Solar To do with the Sun.

Sulphur dioxide A gas produced when coal or oil is burned. It causes environmental pollution.

Turbine A machine with a rotor or paddle that spins when gas or liquid flows through it. For example, turbines driven round by steam are used to turn generators in power stations.

Find out more

www.bbc.co.uk/climate
Look here for everything you need to know about global warming, the evidence for it, what effects it could have in the future, and the Kyoto Agreement.

www.think-energy.com
The site of the Think Energy! campaign, run by British Gas. Clear explanations of different sources of energy and advice and information on saving energy.

www.crest.org
The site of America's Center for Renewable Energy and Sustainable Technology. Excellent and up-to-date information on all forms of renewable energy and energy efficiency, and the latest research.

www.actewagl.com.au/education/electricity/generation
This site is run by actewAGL, Australia's biggest energy supplier. This section includes information about different sources of energy with cartoon diagrams.

www.greenpeace.org
Visit this site to find out about Greenpeace and its campaigns for the environment, including the Clean Energy Now! campaign.

Index

A
Africa 17
atmosphere 8, 10, 12, 21, 30
Australia 11, 31

B
biodegradable waste 20
bioenergy 12, 20–21
bioenergy feedstocks 20, 21
biofuel 21
Brazil 21

C
campaigns 7, 9, 25, 30, 31
Canada 14, 18
carbon dioxide 8, 21, 30
cars 4, 5, 10, 20, 21, 26, 28, 30
clean energy supplies *see
    entry for* renewable energy
    supplies
clean fuels 5

D
dams 18, 19
Denmark 14, 15
diesel fuel 10, 30

E
electricity 6, 7, 11, 17, 30
    from bioenergy feedstocks
        20, 21
    from geothermal energy
        22, 23
    from light 12, 16, 17
    from water 18, 19, 30
    from wind 14, 15
electricity *or* energy
    companies 7, 9, 13, 14
emissions 9, 10, 30
energy efficiency 5, 10, 11,
    24, 25, 26, 30
energy-efficient appliances *or*
    machines 25, 26, 27, 30

energy use 4, 5, 11, 13, 24,
    25, 27, 28, 29, 30
environmental
    damage 4, 5, 6, 24, 30
    laws 7, 24, 30
ethanol 21
European Union (EU) 27

F
flowing water 7, 12, 18, 30
fossil fuels 4, 5, 6, 7, 12, 21,
    30
    burning 6, 7, 8, 9, 10, 13,
        14, 15, 24, 30
France 19
Friends of the Earth
    International (FoEI) 9

G
generator 14, 18, 23, 30
geothermal energy 12, 22–23
Germany 17
global warming 8, 9, 30, 31
grants 25, 30
green energy supplies *see
    entry for* renewable energy
    supplies
greenhouse gases 8, 9, 30
Greenpeace 7, 31
green power schemes 13

H
heating 4, 16, 23, 24, 25
heat insulation 24, 25, 30
hot springs 22, 23
hot water 16, 22, 23
hydroelectricity 7, 12, 18, 19

I, J, K
Iceland 22, 23
industry 8, 11
Japan 9, 14, 17, 22, 23
Kenya 17, 18

Kyoto Agreement 9, 31

L, M, N
lighting 4
manufacturing 11, 28, 29
New Zealand 22
nitrogen oxides 10, 30
non-renewable energy
    supplies 6, 30

P
Philippines, the 19
pollution 5, 6, 11, 21, 30
    reduction 9, 10, 11, 12
power station 6, 7, 14, 15,
    17, 18, 23, 30

R
recycling *and* re-using 24,
    28, 29, 30
refineries 10, 30
renewable energy supplies 5,
    7, 9, 12–13, 14, 20, 23, 30, 31
rivers *and* oceans 18, 19

S
solar cells 12, 16, 17
solar energy 12, 16–17, 30
solar panels 16
South Africa 17
Sri Lanka 21
sulphur dioxide 10, 30
Sun, the 8, 12, 16, 17, 25, 30
Sweden 7

T, U, W
tidal energy 19
turbines 14, 15, 18, 19, 30
UK 14, 20
USA 9, 14, 17, 21, 31
wasting energy 4, 24, 27, 28
wind energy 12, 13, 14–15, 30
wind farms 14, 15